D0742133

DATE DUE

HIGHSMITH #LO-45228

IN THIS SERIES

Auto Racing

Baseball

Basketball

Football

Golf

Hockey

Lacrosse

Soccer

Tennis

Track and Field

Wrestling

THE COMPOSITE GUIDE

to TENNIS

CARRIE MUSKAT

CHELSEA HOUSE PUBLISHERS

Philadelphia

Produced by Choptank Syndicate, Inc.

Editor and Picture Researcher: Norman L. Macht
Production Coordinator and Editorial Assistant: Mary E. Hull
Design and Production: Lisa Hochstein
Cover Illustrator: Cliff Spohn

Cover Design: Keith Trego
Cover Art Direction: Sara Davis
© 1998 by Chelsea House Publishers,
a division of Main Line Book Co.
Printed and bound in the United States of America.

1 3 5 7 9 8 6 4 2

Library of Congress Cataloging-in-Publication Data

Muskat, Carrie.
        The composite guide to tennis / Carrie L. Muskat.
            p.   cm.— (The composite guide)
        Includes bibliographical references (p.) and index.
        Summary: Traces the story of tennis, from its beginnings to its
    first great stars, championships, and notable players of today.
        ISBN 0-7910-4728-8
        1. Tennis—History—Juvenile literature.   2. Tennis players—
    Biography—Juvenile literature. [1. Tennis.]   I. Title.
    II. Series.
    GV996.5.M87 1997
    796.342 — dc21   97-34276
                                                                      CIP
                                                                      AC

CONTENTS

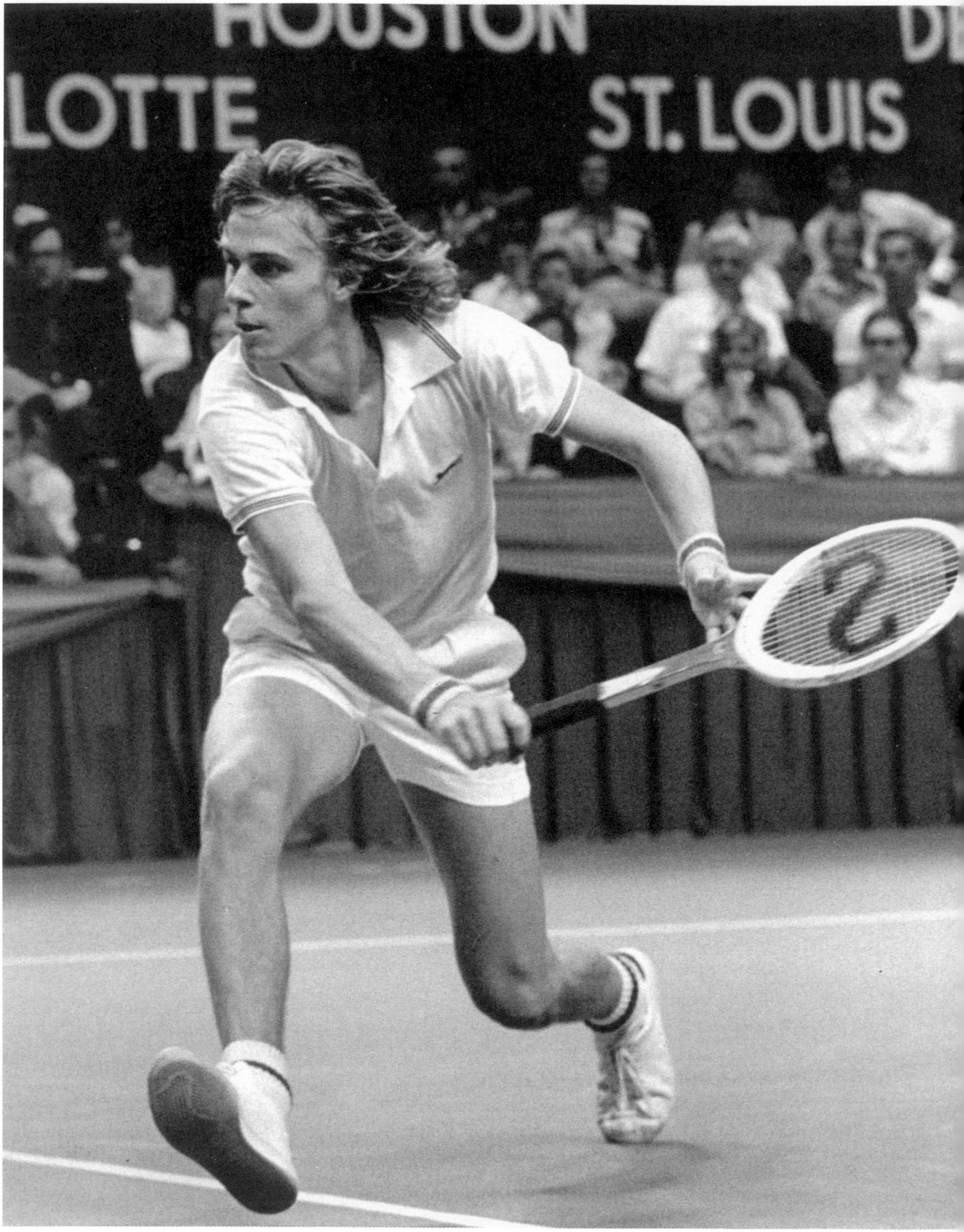
HOUSTON
LOTTE
ST. LOUIS

1

THE BIG GAMES

John McEnroe's reputation as a loud-mouthed brat preceded him into the 1980 Wimbledon final against Bjorn Borg. McEnroe was greeted by a chorus of boos when he walked onto grassy Center Court. Borg was the four-time defending champion.

McEnroe won the first set 6–1, but Borg regained his form and took the second, surviving three break points to win 7–5. Borg took the third 6–3. Tied 4–4 in the fourth, Borg beat McEnroe with a vicious top-spin pass off his two-handed backhand to break serve. In the next game, Borg reached match point twice but McEnroe survived both, saving the second with a risky forehand volley from mid-court.

McEnroe forced the fourth set into a tie-breaker that is remembered for its grittiness. It lasted 20 minutes and consisted of an incredible 34 points. The two seesawed, with Borg on the brink of a championship and McEnroe courageously coming back. The crowd that had booed the brash American was now cheering for him. Six times it went to set point for McEnroe, and then, with McEnroe ahead 17–16, Borg missed a forehand volley and McEnroe punched the air in jubilation. The match was even.

It was tough for Borg to get mentally back into the match and he lost the two opening points on his service, but then everything snapped into place. In a dazzling display of

Bjorn Borg of Sweden won five Wimbledon championships in a row (1976–1980). In 1978 Borg won 49 consecutive matches. But he never won a U.S. Open in 10 attempts.

serving, which allowed McEnroe only one point against it in the entire set, Borg retained his title. After 3 hours 53 minutes of incredible tennis, the final was 1–6, 7–5, 6–3, 6–7, 8–6.

Borg sank to his knees on the grass court, champion for the fifth consecutive year.

Five years earlier, Arthur Ashe had set his mind on Wimbledon. He felt he was the best grass court player who had never won the event. His turn came in 1975. Winning would not be easy. Jimmy Connors, who symbolized a new breed of power player, had emerged in the game, easily winning over Ken Rosewall at Wimbledon in 1974.

In his semifinal match against Roscoe Tanner at Wimbledon, Connors had belted ball after ball into Tanner's court. The harder Tanner hit the ball, the better Connors liked it. He devoured power. Ashe watched the match on television. He knew if he tried to match Connors's power, he would be eaten alive, too. Ashe had tried and lost in previous matches.

So Ashe devised a risky game plan: he would abandon his traditional style and play in a way he never had.

The two men held serve in the first set and Connors led 40–15 on his serve in the third game. Ashe chipped a cross-court return to Connors's forehand and Connors sent the ball into the net. Ashe's game plan kicked in. He dismantled Connors like an engineer defusing a bomb, using gentle, floating shots that made Connors lunge and miss.

Ashe won the first two sets, 6–1, 6–1. He was denying what Connors wanted most and what tennis fans call "pace," which is hard-hit balls. In the third set, though, Ashe made a rare error on an overhead and lost serve. Connors seemed to regain control and won the set 7–5.

But in the fourth set, Ashe regained his composure. He continued to chip and stroke, lob and dink; not until the ninth game did he rip a backhand down the line. He won the next point on another wicked backhand. At 5–4, Ashe was serving for the championship and claimed the trophy with a final forehand volley.

"When I walked on the court, I thought I was going to win," Ashe said later. "I felt it was my destiny."

In 1985, Chris Evert's path to the French Open final included wins over two 15-year-olds,

Arthur Ashe's 1968 U.S. Open victory was the first men's national tennis title won by an African American. After a heart attack forced his retirement in 1980, Ashe became a columnist and civil rights advocate. In 1993 he died of AIDS, which he contracted from an infected blood transfusion.

Steffi Graf and Gabriella Sabatini. But the top-ranked Martina Navratilova waited for Evert in the final on the clay courts. Evert had only one victory in their last 14 meetings and had been soundly defeated 6–3, 6–1 by Navratilova the previous year at the French Open.

"She had killed me the year before," Evert said. "All I remembered was how well she could play on red clay even though it was the surface that gave me the best chance against her."

Evert won the first set 6–3 and led 4–2 in the second. Navratilova found her rhythm and fought back, taking the tiebreaker 7–4 to even the match.

Evert, though, had regained her confidence. She wanted to avoid hitting flat, which allowed Navratilova to chip and come in. So Evert, known as the "Ice Maiden" for her cool composure on the courts, stayed back at the baseline, hitting looping shots.

Evert took a 3–1 lead in the third set, but Navratilova broke back to tie 3–3. Again, Evert fired backhand passes down the line and went ahead 5–3. Navratilova again rallied, allowing only one point out of the next 12 to tie 5–5 and lead 0–40 on Evert's serve. Evert thought she'd blown the match. She went for a winner on the next point and Navratilova missed the forehand volley. That point turned the entire match around. Evert won the match, her sixth French open.

"I was ecstatic," she said. "Beating Martina is always rewarding, but doing it in a Grand Slam final is enough to keep you going for another six months."

It was just one match in an exciting 16-year rivalry between the two friends and powerhouses in women's tennis.

One of the most emotional matches in tennis history occurred in the quarterfinals of the 1995 Australian Open. Pete Sampras had learned midway through the tournament that his coach and longtime friend Tim Gullikson was suffering from brain cancer. Sampras, a stoic player known for his steady play and emotionless demeanor, somehow continued to play. Against Jim Courier in the quarterfinal, Sampras stood in the middle of the court during the fifth set and openly cried. "I started thinking about Tim," Sampras said, "and it just broke my heart." A fan had called out, "Do it for your coach."

Sampras tried to compose himself on the changeover, sobbing into a towel. When he took the court again, he leaned against his racket and continued to cry. Courier, on the other side of the net, was confused. "Are you all right, Pete?" Courier said. "We can do this tomorrow."

But Sampras straightened up and stopped crying. He then served an ace and won the match, 6–7, 6–7, 6–3, 6–4, 6–3.

Andre Agassi defeated Sampras in the final but Sampras was not finished for the season. He beat Boris Becker on Center Court at Wimbledon to become the first player to win three consecutive Wimbledons since Bjorn Borg's run of five from 1976 to 1980. Sampras was only the second to do it since Fred Perry's third in a row in 1936.

"He wasn't the best player in the world today," Agassi said after the Australian final, "but the reality is that he's clearly ahead of everybody."

2

HISTORY OF THE GAME

The origin of the word "tennis" is unclear. Some historians believe the name was derived from various French words. Others trace it to an ancient Egyptian textile center called Tinnis in Arabic, where the linen covers for the tennis balls may have been made.

The game has its origins in Egypt and Persia, and its ancestry includes a 13th-century French game called jeu de paume (game of the hand) which was played with a sheepskin ball and bare hands inside a four-walled room. In 1874, British Major Walter C. Wingfield applied for a patent for a "new and improved portable court for playing the ancient game of tennis." His game was to be played outside on the grass, thus the name "lawn tennis." Wingfield envisioned an hourglass-shaped court, wider at the ends than the middle. A 7-foot-high net would force players to volley the ball, more like badminton.

A British newspaper, *The Field,* detailed the rules of the new game in its March 21, 1874, issue in an article titled "The Major's Game of Lawn Tennis."

The rules have not changed. The size of the court varies depending on whether a singles or doubles match is being played. The court is narrower for singles, wider for doubles. Play begins with a service, each player serving in turn for one game. The first score gained is called 15, the second 30, the third 40, and the fourth is game. If the score becomes 40-all, or

Tennis was an indoor game played primarily by royalty for hundreds of years until lawn tennis made its debut in the 19th century.

deuce, then a player must win two successive points to win the game. A player must win six games to win the set with a margin of at least two games.

A zero score is called "love." The term is probably derived from the French word l'oeuf, meaning "the egg," as in a goose egg.

In 1875, the All England Croquet Club, located in the London suburb of Wimbledon, added lawn tennis to its activities. They designed a court 78 by 27 feet, with the service lines 26 feet from the net, and lowered the net to 3 $1/2$ feet at the center. Later they lowered the net to its present 3 feet and moved the service lines to 21 feet from the net. The All England Club hosted its first championship in July 1877; Spencer Gore defeated William C. Marshall 6–1, 6–2, 6–4. Spectators paid one shilling (about 25 cents) to see the title match.

The All England Club continued to host its lawn tennis championships in Wimbledon, the predecessor to the famous Grand Slam event

Women enjoyed the new game of tennis as much as they could, wearing the long dresses of the 1880s. It would be another 30 years before one woman dared to change the style.

played on grass courts in England each summer. In the 1880s, the Renshaw twins—Willie and Ernest—dominated the singles competition. Willie won the Wimbledon championships 1881–1886 and in 1889, while Ernest won in 1888. The twins, who served hard, volleyed hard, and smashed hard, also dominated the doubles competition, winning in 1880, '81, '84, '85, '86, '88 and '89. Doubles had been introduced in 1879; ladies singles began in 1884. Ladies doubles and mixed doubles did not begin until 1913.

Interest in tennis declined in England around 1890 when people became more interested in two new sports, bicycling and golf.

In January 1874, New Yorker Mary Outerbridge was vacationing in Bermuda. At a local garrison, she saw some British officers playing a strange game using wooden stringed rackets to hit a ball back and forth over a net. Intrigued, she found a colonel who helped outfit her with a complete lawn tennis set. However, when Outerbridge returned to New York with the strange equipment, customs officials stopped her. They could not understand what the young woman was importing.

Mary showed the new game to her brother, A. Emilius Outerbridge, a member of the Staten Island Cricket and Baseball Club. He set up the equipment on a grassy area, gathered a few of his buddies together, and introduced tennis to the United States. Mary's sisters, though, thought the game was unladylike.

About the same time Mary was discovering tennis, Dr. James Dwight of Boston had acquired a net, rackets, and ball from England. He set up a court in Nahant, Massachusetts, a seaside resort north of Boston Harbor and site

The scene at an 1880 tournament on Staten Island, New York.

of the first U.S. tournament in August 1876. That year, Dwight and his cousin Fred Sears handicapped the round-robin tournament for 15 entries. Dwight eventually beat Sears in the final.

In 1878, the Nahant tournament adopted the All England Club rules of the game. However, two years later, Dwight questioned balls used in the tournament, saying they were not proper equipment. The need for uniformity and regulations resulted in the formation of the U.S. National Lawn Tennis Association in 1881. Dwight, called "the father of lawn tennis," became president in 1882, a position he held for 21 years.

The new association sponsored its first national tournament at Newport Casino in Newport, Rhode Island. Twenty-six players entered. Dick Sears, a 19-year-old Harvard student and another of Dwight's cousins, won without losing a set.

In 1884, Dwight competed at Wimbledon, but lost in the second round of singles. He wrote several instructional articles and two books, *Lawn Tennis* (1886) and *Practical Lawn Tennis* (1893). The texts were the standard of instruction until 1920 when Bill Tilden's *The Art of Lawn Tennis* was published.

The same year Dwight played at Wimbledon, 13 women entered the first women's singles competition. Nineteen-year-old Maud Watson defeated her older sister Lilian 6–8, 6–3, 6–3.

In an earlier match, Maud Watson had beaten the Irish women's champion May Langrishe. More than 60 years later the court opponents would be linked in death. In 1939, Langrishe died at a house called "Hammersmead" in Charmouth, a small seaside resort in Devonshire, England. Seven years later, Watson died in the same house.

3 THE PIONEERS

Tennis began as an individual game, but in 1900 it became a team event when Dwight Davis put up the Davis Cup for international team competition. The idea came to him while on a cross-country tennis tour.

Davis, a 21-year-old Harvard graduate, commissioned a $750 sterling silver bowl from a Boston jeweler for first prize. Other members of the first U.S. Davis Cup team were Malcolm Whitman, 23, and Holcombe Ward, 22, who was Davis's doubles partner. Davis was named the U.S. captain for the inaugural event, scheduled for August at the Longwood Cricket Club in Boston.

The British team of Arthur Gore, Ernest Black, and H. Roper Barrett was chosen because they could afford the trip overseas. The American team won handily and, after one year off from competition, repeated as Davis Cup champions in 1902. But in 1903, the British brothers, Reggie and Laurie Doherty, rallied to win, and the Cup left the U.S. for the first time. Laurie Doherty followed his Davis Cup win with a victory in the U.S. National Championship, the first foreigner to win the event.

Wimbledon was growing in stature as one of the top prizes in tennis. May Sutton, a California teenager, entered the event for the first time in 1900, reaching the quarterfinal round that year. In 1904, she won the U.S. singles title and the

Suzanne Lenglen shocked everyone at Wimbledon when she appeared on the court in this outfit in 1919. The 20-year-old French woman won the title and broke the women's dress code forever.

next year, at the age of 18, became the first American woman to win the Wimbledon singles championship.

Tennis had been dominated by club men from wealthy families until Maurice McLoughlin revolutionized the sport with his dynamic serve. He was the first public parks player to win a title, winning the U.S. Championship in 1912. McLoughlin's game emphasized the serve and volley style, in which a player serves, then rushes to the net to play the return before it hits the ground. Nicknamed the "California Comet," McLoughlin made his only appearance at Wimbledon in 1913, flashing his cannon-ball serve. However, he lost to Tony Wilding of New Zealand, the reigning singles champion since 1910.

The site of the U.S. National moved from Newport, R.I., to Forest Hills in Queens, N.Y., in 1913. That year also marked the founding of the International Lawn Tennis Federation (ILTF), now known as the International Tennis Federation. The ILTF membership included clubs and associations around the world.

The United States did not immediately join because it did not like the various "World Championship" titles associated with different events. The ILTF called Wimbledon the "World Championship on Grass," while the Paris tournament was dubbed the "World Championship on Hard Court." The grandiose titles were abolished soon after World War I, and the U.S. then joined the association.

In 1923, a new $250,000 stadium was constructed at the West Side Tennis Club grounds in Forest Hills, N.Y. It opened on August 10 with the inauguration of the Wightman Cup matches. Hazel Hotchkiss

Wightman, a champion in pre–World War I days who competed until she was past 70, had conceived of the idea of a women's competition equivalent to the men's Davis Cup. She donated a silver vase for the event, but the idea stalled for three years.

The first Wightman Cup consisted of five singles matches and two doubles between teams from Great Britain and the United States. Wightman was captain of the American team of Molla Mallory, Helen Wills Moody, and Eleanor Goss that posted a 7–0 victory.

Pro tennis in the late 1920s and 1930s was very different from pro tennis today. Players who declared themselves professionals were banned from competing in ILTF sanctioned events such as Wimbledon and the Davis Cup. The pro tour went from city to city, almost like a circus, and the court had to be set up at each site like a circus tent.

In 1927, the first U.S. Pro Championships were played in New York, giving all the professional players a chance to compete in one tournament. Vinnie Richards won the title, beating Howard Kinsey. The next year, Richards succeeded C.C. "Cash and Carry" Pyle as a promoter of professional matches and imported Czech player Karel Kozeluh. In head-to-head duel with Richards, Kozeluh was superior on clay and hardwood, but lost on grass to Richards in the second U.S. Pro Championships.

Suzanne Lenglen was the pioneer woman in tennis. The daughter of well-to-do Frenchman Charles Lenglen, Suzanne reached the Wimbledon finals in 1919 and created quite a sensation because of her dress. The British were used to seeing women players in tight-fitting corsets, blouses, and layers of petticoats. When Suzanne stepped onto the court, she was wearing a revealing one-piece dress with sleeves just above the elbow. The hemline was just below her knees—quite daring at that time. Some of the women spectators walked out during her matches, shocked at the 20-year-old French-woman's risque appearance. Those who stayed were dazzled by her grace and disciplined shotmaking, and she won the Wimbledon singles title.

Lenglen did more for tennis than any other woman of her time. Tennis writer Al Laney wrote that Lenglen "broke down barriers and created a vogue, reforming tennis dress, substituting acrobatics and something of the art of the ballet where decorum had been the rule. In England and on the Continent, this slim, not very pretty but fascinating French maiden was the most popular performer in sport or out of it on the postwar scene. She became the rage, almost a cult."

In 1921, Lenglen came to America for the first time. In a second-round match at the U.S. National in Forest Hills against defending champion Molla Mallory, Lenglen lost the first set 6–2 and appeared weak and nervous. She lost the first point of the second set, then dou-ble faulted and began crying. She told the umpire she was too sick to continue and defaulted. The crowd of 8,000, the largest ever to watch a women's match in the U.S., hissed in disapproval.

Lenglen avenged the controversial default in the 1922 Wimbledon women's final at the new and present site on Church Road near Wimbledon Common in London. In front of a packed Center Court crowd of 14,750 people, Lenglen beat Mallory 6–2, 6–0.

In 1926, Lenglen was involved in controversy again. She planned to compete in a women's doubles match in front of King George V and Queen Mary of England. But because of a scheduling change, Lenglen arrived after the King and Queen had left. This was considered bad manners and she was reprimanded. The crowds and the press became hostile toward her, and Lenglen eventually lost her doubles match. She withdrew from the tournament. It was her last amateur event.

Lenglen joined American promoter C.C. Pyle and toured the United States, winning all 38 matches against former U.S. champ Mary K. Browne. The tour marked the start of professional tennis as a career.

Suzanne Lenglen died July 4, 1938, from pernicious anemia at the age of 39.

Helen Wills Moody was known as "Little Miss Poker Face" for her stoic expression on the court. She never showed the style or flair that Suzanne Lenglen did. In 1928, Moody won both at Wimbledon and Forest Hills for the second straight year and also won the French title. A *New York Herald Tribune* reporter wrote, "She plays her game with a silent deadly earnestness, concentrated on her work. That, of course, is the way to win games but it does not please galleries."

Despite all her success, Moody is remembered most for a match she lost. In 1933, she had six Wimbledon titles and seven U.S. titles to her credit. Only rival Helen Jacobs stood in the way of an eighth championship at Forest Hills. Jacobs won her first set ever against

Helen Wills Moody won seven national singles titles in the 1920s. She was so absorbed in her game while on the court, writers called her "Little Miss Poker Face," because she showed no expression.

Moody, 8–6, to start the match, dominating with her net play. Jacobs led 3–0 in the second set when Moody walked over to the umpire's chair, put her sweater on, and announced she could not play. Her back pain was too much to bear. Jacobs asked if Moody simply needed some rest, but Moody said no and left the court without even shaking hands. The press accused Moody of being a quitter and a poor sport.

Moody was upset at having spoiled the National Championships, but she said she should have listened to her doctor's advice and not entered the event. It was Moody's first loss since she had been beaten by Lenglen in 1926.

Moody finished with a record eight Wimbledon titles (surpassed by Martina Navratilova's nine in 1990) in nine tries. From 1927 to 1932, she did not lose a set in singles anywhere.

4   THE FIRST STARS

William "Big Bill" Tilden came of age in 1920 when he won at Wimbledon and Forest Hills and helped the U.S. team win the Davis Cup for the first time since 1913. Tilden fell behind in all three sets of his Wimbledon final against Zenzo Shimizu of Japan, but rallied to win in all three. Some observers felt Tilden was toying with his opponent. He beat Bill Johnston in a dramatic five-set final, 6–1, 1–6, 7–5, 5–7, 6–3, to win the U.S. championship. During the match, a Navy photographic plane crashed while making passes over Forest Hills and disrupted the match for a short time. It was the first of six consecutive national titles for the flamboyant Tilden, who would not lose another important match until 1926.

Standing more than 6 feet tall with big shoulders, Tilden had speed, nimbleness, coordination, and perfect balance. The son of a Philadelphia wool merchant, he also was a bit of a rebel. In 1924, he sent a letter of resignation to the USTA, saying he could not compete in the Davis Cup because of a proposed ban on his writing for newspapers about tennis. The USTA felt it was a conflict of amateur rules. The association eventually gave in to Tilden's demands because they needed the talented player on the team, and he and Bill Johnston swept the Australians 5–0.

A showman as well as a skilled baseline player with a cannonball serve, the 6' 2" Bill Tilden was named the greatest tennis player of all time in 1969.

Tilden won 57 consecutive games during the summer of 1925 and captured the U.S. Championship again with a five-set victory over Johnston. It was the last of Tilden's six straight U.S. titles and the last time he and Johnston would compete in what had become the battle between "Big Bill" and "Little Bill." Tilden lost in the quarterfinals the next year to Frenchman Henri Cochet, 6–8, 6–1, 6–3, 1–6, 8–6, ending his record U.S. run of 42 matches.

In 1931 Tilden revived pro tennis, which had languished since its inception in 1926 when Suzanne Lenglen went on tour. Tilden was co-promoter of his tour and opened against Karel Kozeluh of Czechoslovakia at Madison Square Garden in New York on February 18, 1931, before a crowd of 13,000. Tilden won 6–4, 6–2, 6–4, then ran off 16 consecutive victories on his cross-country tour, grossing $238,000.

Tilden toured the country in 1932 and '33, but the Depression was on and tennis needed new blood. Young Ellsworth Vines joined Tilden's tour and beat the master 47–26 in matches that year. Tilden remained an attraction and for years he traveled across the country, sometimes driving all night to reach a city. He even had to help set up the courts at some sites.

Fred Perry turned pro late in 1936 after dominating tennis the four previous years. He had won three successive Wimbledon titles, three U.S. titles, a French and an Australian title, and nine out of 10 Davis Cup challenge round matches as an amateur. Born in Stockport, England, in 1909, Perry did not take up tennis until he was 18 years old. He developed an undercut backhand, and although he was not overpowering with his strokes, he was an aggressive player, constantly challenging his opponent.

Huge crowds turned out to see him take on Ellsworth Vines and Bill Tilden on the pro tour. Perry won the U.S. Pro Championships in 1938 and 1941.

Don Budge, a 6' 2" redhead from Oakland, California, made his mark in tennis in 1938 when he became the first to win the Grand

British-born Fred Perry won three consecutive Wimbledon titles in the 1930s, then became a U.S. professional champion.

Don Budge was the first to win the grand slam of tennis: the Australian, French, and U.S. Nationals and Wimbledon. One opponent said of Budge, "Playing tennis against him was like playing against a concrete wall." Others called him the finest player who ever lived.

Slam. That year, Budge had rejected offers to turn pro because he felt a loyalty to help the U.S. team in the Davis Cup competition. Enjoying his best season ever on the amateur circuit, Budge won the Australian final, the French championship, Wimbledon, and the U.S. championship at Forest Hills, a feat never before accomplished.

Budge then left the amateur ranks with the blessing of USTA president Holcombe Ward and Davis Cup captain Walter L. Pate. He made his pro debut at Madison Square Garden in New York early in 1939 before a crowd of 16,725 and defeated Ellsworth Vines 6–3, 6–4, 6–2. Budge then defeated Vines 21–18 and Fred Perry 18–11 on the tour.

Truly an all-around player, Budge was known for his powerful serve, solid backhand, and aggressive net play. He defeated Bobby Riggs 6–2, 6–2, 6–2 for the U.S. Pro title at

Alice Marble dominated women's tennis in the late 1930s. Later she pressured tennis officials to allow Althea Gibson to compete in national tournaments, and she coached Billie Jean King.

Forest Hills in 1942, then enlisted in the Air Force. After the war, Budge could not revive his career because of a shoulder injury suffered in military training, although he did reach the U.S. Pro final in 1946, '47, '49 and '53.

"I consider him the finest player 365 days a year who ever lived," Tilden once said.

The pro tour was a bust during World War II. In 1942, the tour played 71 cities, drawing only 101,915 customers. In the 1950s and '60s, Jack Kramer organized a popular men's pro tour. But the ILTF still refused to accept professional players at its events, despite the fact that many promoters paid amateur players not only fees but also living expenses to compete in events. That system changed in 1968.

5 POSTWAR GROWTH

Despite the popularity of professional barnstorming tours featuring such stars as Suzanne Lenglen, Bill Tilden, and Don Budge, tennis did not become a true professional sport until 1968. That year signaled the beginning of what is known as the Open Era of tennis.

Amateur and professional players rarely faced each other on the same court. Once players signed a professional contract, they were automatically banned from competing at Wimbledon or any other event held under the auspices of the International Lawn Tennis Federation (ILTF).

In 1967 Texas oilman Lamar Hunt founded World Championship Tennis (WCT), a Dallas-based professional organization that precipitated the birth of Open tennis. Hunt had signed eight of the top men's players to contracts, calling them the "Handsome Eight." The players included Dennis Ralston, Butch Buchholz, John Newcombe, Tony Roche, Nikki Pilic, Cliff Drysdale, Pierre Barthes, and Roger Taylor.

During the early years, the WCT was considered by many players to be the best run and most respected tour in the game. It was shocking to traditionalists. The players wore bright colors, not pure white as required at Wimbledon, and they encouraged the crowd to cheer.

As more players signed up with the WCT—including 1967 Wimbledon champion Newcombe—Herman David, chairman of the All England

Barred from playing on public courts because she was African American, Althea Gibson won 10 straight black tournaments from 1947 through 1956. When the bars were lowered, Gibson won the 1957 Wimbledon and U.S. Nationals, as well as doubles championships in each.

Club, became concerned that Wimbledon would lose the top caliber players. He boldly announced that he was going to run a professional tennis tournament for amateur and professional players alike on the sacred Center Court at Wimbledon in August 1968.

At the first "pro" Wimbledon, 13 former champions were in the field, which was so strong that Newcombe was relegated to the No. 4 seed in the men's singles. Don Budge and Bobby Riggs, both pre-war champions and pioneers of the professional game, had been unable to compete at Wimbledon once they turned pro. Now both came back. But "Rocket" Rod Laver won the event, beating Tony Roche in the finals to receive $4,800 for the championship.

Some players wanted to maintain their amateur status to compete in the Davis Cup. Lawn Tennis Associations around the world still opposed pro tennis, but they allowed some of the men to register as "authorized" players. An authorized player could accept prize money. An amateur could not.

One such amateur was Arthur Ashe, surprise winner of the 1968 U.S. Open, who beat Tom Okker in five sets. Okker, an authorized player under the Dutch Lawn Tennis Association, accepted $14,000 in prize money for second place. Ashe, an amateur, got nothing.

The men's tour added another incentive in 1970. Jack Kramer, who had organized pro barnstorming tours in the 1950s and '60s, devised the Grand Prix tournament concept, in which players would earn the right to compete for top prize money at year's end by accumulating points in designated tournaments. In 1970, Pepsi sponsored the first Grand Prix

John Newcombe, the 1967 Wimbledon champion, was the best of the original eight men to join the World Championship Tennis professional organization, which opened all tournaments to pro players.

Masters, with first place worth $25,000. Six years later, first place earned $150,000. In 1987, Ivan Lendl received $800,000 for finishing first.

The first and only major rule change in pro tennis occurred in 1971 when officials added the tiebreaker system. When a set ends tied at six games, players square off in a best-of-9-points tiebreaker. The rule was altered in 1979 to a 12-point tiebreaker. The year 1971 also was significant for the players. In the fall, the ILTF, upset that the WCT was so successful and luring all the top players, altered its ruling regarding pro players and passed a resolution banning WCT pros from all tournaments, effective January 1972. The players objected. At the 1972 U.S. Open, they created the Association of Tennis Professionals (ATP). Cliff Drysdale was the first president and found himself in the middle of a controversy almost immediately.

Nikki Pilic did not play for his native Yugoslav team in the Davis Cup competition, saying he had signed a contract that stated his participation was strictly conditional. The Yugoslav Federation suspended him for nine months. The International Lawn Tennis Federation heard Pilic's case and reduced the suspension to one month, but the timing was such that he would not be able to compete in Wimbledon in 1973. After lengthy meetings and attempts at compromise, the ATP players decided to boycott Wimbledon.

Bickering among the various governing factions continued to plague men's pro tennis. Eventually, the ATP created its own 16-event tour, starting in 1990.

The issue wasn't money. The players wanted a tour structured so they didn't have to compete in Tokyo one week and Paris the next. They wanted stronger fields. "What we are trying to do is present a better image of tennis to the public, so they will see more big matches between the top players," said pro player John McEnroe.

Meanwhile, women's pro tennis players had gone their own way. The female players celebrate September 23, 1970, as the birthdate for their pro game. That year, Margaret Court became only the second woman to capture a Grand Slam, winning the French, Wimbledon, U.S., and Australian championships. She earned just $15,000 for the four-tournament feat.

Tennis's top women players wanted a fair share of the pie. The "Open Era" of tennis meant tournaments were finally offering prize money. But the women were playing for only a fraction of what was available to the men. Rod Laver received $8,000 for winning the 1968 Wimbledon men's singles championship while Billie Jean King, the women's singles champion, received less than $3,000.

The discrepancy became ridiculous at the Pacific Southwest Championships in Los Angeles in 1970. The men's singles champion received $12,500 while the women's champion got only $1,500. Any woman who did not reach the quarterfinal round would not earn a single cent. The women also had to cover their own expenses while the men did not.

King and Rosie Casals were the first to protest. They asked Gladys Heldman, founder of *World Tennis* magazine, to negotiate with Jack Kramer, the Pacific Southwest promoter, on behalf of the women players. That did not work, so Heldman decided to help the women organize a boycott of the tournament. She put up $5,000 of her own money to stage a women's tournament that same week at the Houston Racquet Club in Houston, Texas.

Heldman called on Joseph F. Cullman III, then-CEO of Philip Morris Inc., who contributed another $2,500 to the purse on behalf of Virginia Slims, his new women's cigarette. The cigarette's slogan: "You've Come a Long Way, Baby."

On September 23, 1970, at Heldman's home in Houston, nine players signed symbolic $1 contracts and the Virginia Slims Circuit was born. The "Original Nine" were Peaches Bartkowicz, Rosie Casals, Julie M. Heldman, Billie Jean King, Kristy Pigeon, Nancy Richey, and Val Zeigenfuss, from the U.S., plus Australians Judy Dalton and Kerry Melville.

The Virginia Slims tournament began that afternoon. The next day, the USLTA notified the American players by telegram that their memberships had been suspended. That meant they could not be ranked and could not play in the Grand Slam tournaments, Wightman Cup, or Federation Cup competition. The women were unfazed.

Rosie Casals won that first Virginia Slims in Houston and the $1,600 first prize, beating Judy Dalton in the final.

"We had all won that week," King said. "Women's tennis would never be the same."

By 1971, the Virginia Slims circuit expanded to tournaments in 19 cities and the women were competing for $309,100 in prize money. Other companies, including the Ford Motor Co. and Kmart, joined in sponsoring the new women's pro circuit. The USLTA tried to lure the women players back, agreeing that the players could skip any tournaments that did not meet the miminum prize money standards. It was not a comfortable situation.

In September 1971, the women returned to Houston to celebrate their one-year anniversary with a $40,000 event. Billie Jean King won the $10,000 first prize, the largest ever awarded to a woman tennis player. King set another milestone in 1971 by becoming the first woman athlete to reach $100,000 in prize money in a single year.

By 1972, the "Original Nine" had grown to 60 players and prize money had increased to $600,000. The season ended with the first Tour Championships, offering a total purse of $100,000. The next year, the USLTA sponsored

Billie Jean King was a leader in the fight to gain equal treatment and prize money for women. Pledged to change the "rich . . . white . . . male" world of tennis, in 1973 she defeated Bobby Riggs in the "Battle of the Sexes" before a crowd of 30,472 and a national television audience.

Margaret Court won the four Grand Slam tournaments—Wimbledon and the French, Australian, and U.S. Opens—in 1970, and retired with a record total of 66 wins in those events.

a rival tour featuring new stars Chris Evert and Evonne Goolagong but offering much less prize money. The Slims tour offered a total of $775,000 at tournaments in 22 cities that year. By the end of 1973, the two tours merged into one with Virginia Slims still the main sponsor.

In July 1973, Billie Jean King gathered 62 women players in a conference room at the Gloucester Hotel in London to organize their own players association, creating the Women's Tennis Association (WTA). King was elected the first president.

The impact was immediate. At the 1973 U.S. Open, for the first time in a major tournament, the women played for a purse equal to the men's. Margaret Court captured the $25,000 first prize.

In 1978, a political struggle emerged between the WTA and Virginia Slims, and the women elected to establish a new circuit with a new sponsor, Avon. Virginia Slims resumed sponsorship in 1983—with the WTA's approval—but did not host a Virginia Slims Championship at year's end until 1984. However, the sponsorship came under fire because of the link with cigarettes, an unhealthy product. Kraft General Foods took over sponsorship in 1991.

Corel Corporation, a world leader in computer graphics and CD-ROM technology, became the tour's title sponsor in 1996, offering $36 million in prize money at 55 tournaments around the world.

Women's tennis had indeed come a long way.

6   **MODERN STARS**

Jimmy Connors was a very brash and very confident tennis player. He grew up in Belleville, Illinois, under the tutelage of his mother, Gloria, who was a tennis teaching pro. Connors made up for his small stature with determination and grit. He turned pro in 1972 and won his first title that year in Jacksonville, Florida.

"My mother rolled balls to me and I swung at them," said Connors, who was just 2 years old when he first picked up a racket. "I held the racket with both hands because that was the only way I could lift it."

In 1974, Connors, then 23, beat Ken Rosewall first at Wimbledon and again in the U.S. Open, and his manager claimed Connors was the "heavyweight champion of tennis." Connors personified power tennis. He took over the No. 1 spot in the rankings in July 1974 and held it 160 consecutive weeks. A lefty who pummeled opponents with his two-fisted backhand, he competed through the 1992 season, when he was 41 years old.

The 1991 season was his most remarkable. Connors's career had seemed over after an elbow injury the previous year, which limited him to three losing matches. He dropped to No. 936 in the rankings. After surgery and an intensive rehabilitation, Connors came back to play in 14

Chris Evert and Martina Navratilova were fierce competitors for 16 years. Called the "Ice Maiden" because of her unemotional style on the court, Evert won the French Open for the sixth time in 1985, defeating Navratilova.

tournaments, ending with a fantastic semifinal finish at the U.S. Open.

Connors has played and won more tournaments and matches than any other male pro. He triumphed at the U.S. Open, winning five championships, and he won Wimbledon twice and the Australian Open once.

Bjorn Borg was a new breed of player, a fleet-footed athlete who could run all day and who relied on his stamina, speed, concentration, and topspin. He remained his own man, conducting himself in a quiet professional style rather than getting caught up in the flashy '70s. Borg, known for his trademark headband and long blonde hair, was the youngest winner of the Italian Championship and the French Championship, winning both prior to his 18th birthday. He adapted his two-handed backhand from hockey, a game he preferred to play as a child in his native Sweden. Born in 1956 in Sodertalje, Sweden, Borg was fascinated with a tennis racket his father had won as a prize in a Ping-Pong tournament.

A tireless baseline player, Borg changed his style prior to Wimbledon in 1976, concentrating on serve-and-volley tactics better suited to the grass courts. The hard work paid off and he won that year without losing a set, taking the championship over favored Ilie Nastase. Borg was the youngest champion of the modern era at 20 years one month until Boris Becker won in 1985 at the age of 17.

Borg went on to win five consecutive Wimbledons, including the brilliant victory over John McEnroe in 1980 that included the 34-point tiebreaker. But McEnroe ended Borg's bid for a sixth in '81, winning in four sets.

Borg did not have the same luck at the U.S. Open, failing to win in 10 tries. He lost four finals, twice to Connors and twice to McEnroe.

Born in 1954 in Fort Lauderdale, Florida, Chris Evert made a grand debut at the age of 15, beating the No. 1 player in the world, Margaret Court, at a small tournament in North Carolina. A year later, Evert became the youngest to reach the semifinals of the U.S. Open at 16 years 8 months 20 days, but she lost to eventual champion Billie Jean King.

A baseline specialist, Evert beat her opponents with metronomic strokes that seldom missed. Her father, Jimmy Evert, had advised her against using a two-handed backhand, but it became a key part of Evert's game. "She started that way because she was too small and

Jimmy Connors won more men's singles titles through 1996 than any other player—109. Early in his career, Connors often fought with courtside judges and umpires, officials, and other players before he mellowed.

weak to swing the backhand with one hand," Jimmy Evert said. "I hoped she'd change—but how can I argue with this success?"

Evert was the first women's player to reach $1 million in career prize money, doing so in 1976. She won at least one major singles title for 13 consecutive years, beginning in 1974 and ending in 1986 at the French Open.

But Evert is better known for her friendly rivalry with Martina Navratilova. From 1973 to 1988, the two played 80 matches. They first met

The terrible-tempered John McEnroe earned the nick-name "Superbrat" for his sulking and outbursts against officials during tournaments. His behavior overshadowed his skill with the racket. In 1984, he won 82 out of 85 matches.

on an indoor court in Akron, Ohio, in 1973. Evert won that first-round match 7–6, 6–3. It was not until their sixth meeting, the quarterfinals of the Virginia Slims of Washington, that Martina would defeat Chris.

Navratilova rallied, winning nine of 13 of their major final engagements and 43 of the 80 head-to-head matches.

Evert's consistency in both her style of play and ability to win was criticized as being monotonous. "I realize that a lot of fans think my game is boring and they want to see me lose or at least for somebody to give me a good fight all the time," she said. "But this is the game I played to win. Losing hurts me. I was always determined to be the best."

She was the No. 1 player in the world in 1975, '76, '77, '80 and '81. Evert was the first player to win more than 1,000 singles matches as well as 150 tournaments. Her 55-match winning streak in 1974, which ended at the U.S. Open, was an Open Era record until Navratilova won 74 in a row in 1984.

Born in Prague, Czechoslovakia, in 1956, Martina Navratilova first attracted notice at the age of 16 when she reached the quarterfinals of the French Open, defeating the former champion Nancy Richey. Her aggressive serve and volley style was a sharp contrast to that of most women players who stayed on the baseline, and it was well-suited to doubles.

Her Wimbledon records include nine consecutive final appearances from 1982–1990 and 108 match wins. Navratilova also has won four U.S., three Australian, and two French singles for a total of 18 majors, tying her with Evert.

7

RECORD SETTERS

Martina Navratilova may not have completed the Grand Slam in a single year, but she established herself as the greatest women's player ever in the record books. Navratilova holds a record 167 singles titles, more than any other male or female player, and won at least one tour event a year for 21 consecutive years. From her debut in 1973 until she retired in November 1994, Navratilova compiled a 1,438–212 match record (.872 winning percentage) and earned more than $20 million.

A devoted fitness enthusiast, Navratilova showed she still had plenty of life in her at the 1993 Paris Indoor tournament when she defeated Monica Seles in a third-set tiebreaker to become the oldest player—at 36—to defeat a current No. 1 player.

Margaret Court leads all women players with 24 Grand Slam titles, Helen Wills Moody won 19, and Navratilova won 18.

Navratilova did complete a non-calendar year "Grand Slam," beginning with the 1983 Wimbledon to the 1984 U.S. Open, tieing Court's record of six consecutive Grand Slam victories. Court, an Australian, won 62 singles titles and captured the Grand Slam itself in 1970.

From January 16 to December 6, 1984, Navratilova set the longest consecutive match win streak at 74, breaking Chris Evert's mark of 55. The powerful Czechoslovakian-born left-hander

Martina Navratilova of Czechoslovakia may have been the greatest tennis player of either sex. She holds the most records, including 167 singles championships. In 1983 she lost only once in 87 tournaments.

also won more money that year than all athletes in the world except for three boxers, pocketing $2,173,556. The No. 1 player in the world for 332 weeks, Navratilova also dominated the doubles events. She won singles and doubles titles at the same event 84 times to lead all players.

The only women to win the Grand Slam were Maureen Connolly in 1953, Court in 1970, and Steffi Graf in 1988. Graf is the first woman player to win each of the four Grand Slam singles titles at least four times, and the only player, male or female, to win all four Grand Slam singles crowns in the '90s. Through 1995, she had won a minimum of seven tournaments a year for 10 years.

Graf also was ranked the No. 1 player for a record 186 consecutive weeks, from August 17, 1987, to March 10, 1991, longer than any player, male or female. Jimmy Connors holds the men's record of 160 weeks, from July 29, 1974, to August 16, 1977.

Maureen Connolly became the first woman Grand Slam winner in 1953. Nicknamed "Little Mo," she dominated the game from the baseline. The Californian lost only one set in winning the Grand Slam. That year, she won 10 of 12 tournaments with a 61–2 match record. A freak accident ended her career prematurely. Connolly was injured when a horse she was riding was hit by a truck, causing a serious leg injury. She died of cancer at the age of 34 in 1969. The previous year, Connolly was inducted into the tennis Hall of Fame.

Margaret Court is the only player, male or female, to win the Grand Slam in both singles and doubles. She won the mixed doubles Slam in 1963 with Ken Fletcher and won the singles titles at the four majors in 1970. The most prolific winner of major championships prior to Navratilova, Court won 62 titles in singles, doubles, and mixed doubles between 1960 and '75.

Court was remarkable in that she continued to win major titles, including the U.S. Open in 1973, after the birth of the first of three children. She was still competing at 34. During her Grand Slam year, Court won 21 of 27 tournaments with a 104–6 match record and earned $14,800 for the four titles. Graf took home $877,724 when she won the Grand Slam in 1988.

Don Budge and Rod Laver are the only male players to win the Grand Slam. Budge was the first among all players, capturing the Australian, French, Wimbledon, and U.S. Open in 1938. Laver, known as "The Rocket," won all four singles titles in 1962 and again in 1969.

Laver was born a little more than one month before Budge completed the first Grand Slam. An incessant attacker, Laver's game was guided by his strong left arm, which was able to create a nasty topspin by brushing the ball from low to high. It created a high bounce and was difficult to volley. In 1969, Laver enjoyed one of the finest years on the courts, winning an Open Era record 17 singles tournaments out of 32 entered and compiling a 106–16 match record. In 1962, he had won 19 of 34 tournaments with a 134–15 record.

His second Grand Slam was more impressive because both pros and amateur players were included in the field following the advent of Open tennis in 1968. The Australian was the first player to earn $1 million. During his

23-year career, he won 47 pro titles in singles and finished runner-up in 22.

Fifteen years after Laver won his second Slam, John McEnroe enjoyed the best season in 1984, compiling an 82–3 record and .965 winning percentage, tops among men. He could have improved upon that mark that year if he had not lost his temper in the final of the French Open against Ivan Lendl. He led Lendl 2–0 in sets only to be distracted by his outbursts and beaten in five sets.

Jimmy Connors also was a fiery player and holds the record for most career singles titles with 109. Beginning in 1974, he played in five

Rod "Rocket" Laver's powerful topspin drives enabled him to become the only person ever to win the Grand Slam twice.

successive U.S. Open finals, the first man to do so since Bill Tilden from 1918 to 1925. Connors finished with a 98–17 record at the U.S. Open.

In terms of pure guts and dramatics, Pete Sampras may have set the record on September 5, 1996, at the U.S. Open. Sampras and Spaniard Alex Corretja clashed in a quarterfinal match that lasted 4 hours 9 minutes. Doubled over by the effects of dehydration, Sampras staggered around the baseline after Game 2 of the tiebreaker and then vomited on the court. A ball boy offered a white towel, then carefully wiped up the small puddle. By Game 7, Sampras was using his racket as a makeshift cane between points to support himself. The match finally ended when Corretja double faulted on the 16th point of a fifth-set tiebreaker.

At the end, Sampras was so exhausted he could not lift his arms in triumph. He said he drew his strength from the memory of his coach and longtime friend Tim Gullikson, who had died of cancer earlier in the year.

"This one's for Tim," Sampras said after the match. "Tim was there for me."

Sampras, who grew up idolizing Laver, would go on to win his fourth U.S. Open title, and eighth Grand Slam tournament, with a victory over Michael Chang.

8

THE FUTURE

When Martina Navratilova retired in November 1994, most of the players on the women's tour breathed a sigh of relief. But a new Martina emerged as an integral part of tennis's future.

Martina Hingis started playing tennis at the age of 2 when her mother, Melanie Molitor, would hit balls to her every day for 10 minutes. Hingis, who was named after Navratilova, was a natural. She broke into the top 20 just eight months after playing her first WTA Tour event, and in 1995 became the youngest player in the Open era to win a singles match at the Australian Open at just 14 years 4 months.

At 16, she became the youngest to reach the No. 1 ranking when she defeated Monica Seles at the Lipton Championships in April 1997. "Why should I be worried about the future?" Hingis said after her Lipton victory. "Right now, almost everything is perfect." Hingis is one of the most outrageous players to burst onto the scene. She likes to go rollerblading between matches of a tournament and if not on her 'blades, she can usually be found riding horses.

A fresh face can only bolster the women's tour, which was revived briefly in 1995 with the return of Monica Seles. Seles was stabbed in the back during a changeover at a tournament in Hamburg, Germany, in 1993 and did not return

A bright new star burst onto the tennis scene when 16-year-old Martina Hingis became the youngest ever to gain top-seeded ranking in 1997.

to the tour until 27 $^1/_2$ months later when she won the 1995 Canadian Open.

The WTA Tour was televised in more than 130 countries and reached nearly 6.1 billion homes in 1995. Prize money in 1996 totaled more than $36 million, a vast improvement from 1970 when women pro players were fighting for far less than their male counterparts. In 1995, more than 70 women players earned six-figure incomes on the tour, and more than 60 players in the tour's history have surpassed the $1 million mark in career earnings.

The women's tour traveled to 25 countries for 11 months of the year. Some 500 players representing 45 different countries competed in 1996.

In 1995, the prize money for the men's ATP tour totaled a record $64 million. Worldwide attendance exceeded 4 million for the first time in 1994. The men played in 85 tournaments in 38 countries on six continents.

But both the men's and women's tours recognized the need to offer more than just tennis matches. They added to the tournament atmosphere by creating fan-friendly innovations such as the ATP Tour FanFest, a miniature tennis theme park that traveled from site to site.

The rankings by the ATP and the WTA credit players with a certain number of points depending on how far they get in each tournament. Additional points are awarded when a player beats someone ranked in the top 75. The rankings then help tournament directors determine the seeds.

However, tennis may someday discover it could attract more interest if it loosened up a little. World Team Tennis, the brainchild of

Billie Jean King, established city team franchises, played rock and roll music during matches, urged players to wear bright colors and used a Ping-Pong scoring system, not traditional tennis scoring. At its high point in 1974, the WTT included most of the game's leading players. But the WTT folded after five years because of financial losses.

Tennis has been marketed well by such sporting giants as Nike. Professionals Andre

Pete Sampras was only 19 when he won the U.S. Open championship in 1990. With a serve once timed at 130 miles an hour, the quiet Sampras reached top ranking in 1993. He played in some of the most dramatic matches of the 1990s.

Agassi, Monica Seles, and Pete Sampras were among Nike's superstar clients. The shoe and clothing company jazzed up Agassi's outfits in hopes that people other than tennis players would buy them.

Turner Broadcasting, which owned the Cartoon Network, and the Tennis Industry Association banded together in an advertising and promotional campaign to get youngsters onto the courts. The commercials showed real children playing tennis with cartoon characters like Tom and Jerry or Scooby Doo. The campaign included a joint promotion called Cartoon Network/Smash Tennis, which set up at tournament sites across the country. People dressed as cartoon characters were available to hit tennis balls on an inflatable tennis court with kids attending the matches.

The game continued to look for ways to increase interest. Once considered the yuppie sport of choice, it had been replaced in popularity by golf. The popularity of tennis peaked in 1978 when 35 million Americans played the game. In 1996, fewer than 20 million picked up a racket.

The Tennis Industry Association was formed to join forces with the U.S. Tennis Association to sponsor "Play Tennis America," a program of free lessons aimed at getting adults to try the game. But they know that the future of tennis depended on encouraging youngsters to pick up a racket.

But the most powerful promotion for the sport was the success of its latest young superstars. Following their 1997 Wimbledon victories, both Martina Hingis and Pete Sampras were poised to break many tennis records.

At 16, Hingis breezed through the prestigious tournament to become the youngest Wimbledon winner in the 20th century. She had lost only one match out of 45 for the year. Soon after that triumph, she won the U.S. Open as well.

Sampras, 25, won with equal ease in becoming the first American to win four times at Wimbledon. It was his 10th Grand Slam victory, tying him with the pioneer American pro, Bill Tilden. Young by normal standards but old as tennis stars go (at 26 Bjorn Borg and John McEnroe had won their last major titles), the versatile Sampras looked forward to competing on the courts for years to come.

Neither young star was ready to slow down, despite having achieved tennis's most cherished goal so early in their careers. Helen Wills Moody, an eight-time Wimbledon champion, described the experience: "The dream nearest a player's heart is that of winning a title at historic Wimbledon, to have one's name inscribed on the shields that carry those of the winners from the very first, when tennis was new."

CHRONOLOGY

1877 – The All England Croquet Club, located in the London suburb of Wimbledon, hosts its first lawn tennis championship, the predecessor to Wimbledon, in July.

1881 – First men's U.S. Championship played at Newport Casino, Newport, R.I., predecessor to the U.S. Open, sponsored by newly created U.S. National Lawn Tennis Association.

1900 – Dwight Davis commissions $750 silver bowl as prize in first Davis Cup competition.

1905 – First men's Australian Championships played, predecessor to Australian Open.

1913 – International Lawn Tennis Federation founded.

1923 – New $250,000 stadium opens at Forest Hills, New York; first Wightman Cup competition, the women's equivalent of the Davis Cup.

1925 – First men's and women's French Championships played, predecessor to French Open.

1933 – Australian Vivian McGrath uses a two-handed backhand at Wimbledon and British player Bunny Austin wears shorts for the first time on Center Court.

1938 – Don Budge, 23, becomes the first to win the four major championships—Australia, France, Wimbledon, and the U.S.—a feat that becomes known as the Grand Slam.

1967 – Texas oilman Lamar Hunt creates World Championship Tennis tour for men players.

1968 – The "Open Era" of tennis begins with professionals allowed to enter tournaments.

1970 – Promoter Jack Kramer creates Grand Prix tour for men; women's Virginia Slims Circuit formed.

1972 – Male players form Association of Tennis Professionals (ATP).

1973 – Female players create their own Women's Tennis Association (WTA).

1978 – U.S. Open moves to Flushing Meadow, N.Y.

MAJOR RECORDS

GRAND SLAM WINNERS – SINGLES

Don Budge, 1938
Maureen Connolly, 1953
Rod Laver, 1962 & 1969
Margaret Smith Court, 1970
Steffi Graf, 1988

GRAND SLAM EVENTS – ALL-TIME CHAMPIONS
(singles, doubles, mixed doubles combined)

WOMEN		MEN	
Margaret Court	66 titles	Roy Emerson	28 titles

CAREER SINGLES TITLES

WOMEN		MEN	
Martina Navratilova	167	Jimmy Connors	109

BEST ANNUAL WIN-LOSS RECORDS SINCE 1980

WOMEN		MEN	
Martina Navratilova	86–1 .989 (1983)	John McEnroe	82–3 .965 (1984)

LONGEST WIN STREAKS – SINGLES

WOMEN		MEN	
Martina Navratilova	74 matches (1984)	Bjorn Borg	49 matches (1978)

MOST CONSECUTIVE WEEKS AT NO. 1

WOMEN		MEN	
Steffi Graf	186 weeks	Jimmy Connors	160 weeks

FURTHER READING

Baltzell, E. Digby. *Sporting Gentlemen: Men's Tennis from the Age of Honor to the Cult of the Superstar.* New York: Free Press, 1995.

Collins, Bud and Zander, Hollander, eds. *Tennis Encyclopedia.* Detroit: Invisible Ink Press, 1997.

Quackenbush, Robert. *Arthur Ashe and His Match with History.* New York: Simon & Schuster, 1994.

Sanford, William R. and R. Green. *Billie Jean King.* New York: Crestwood House, 1993.

INDEX

PICTURE CREDITS National Archives: pp. 2, 24, 30, 60; The International Tennis Hall of Fame & Museum, Newport, RI: pp. 6, 9, 12, 29, 35, 39, 42, 45, 48, 52; Library of Congress: pp. 14, 16; Boston Public Library: pp. 18, 26, 31, 32; Archive Photos: pp. 40, 54; UPI/Corbis-Bettmann: p. 46; AP/Wide World: p. 57

CARRIE MUSKAT has covered major league baseball since 1981, beginning with United Press International in Minneapolis. She was UPI's lead writer at the 1991 World Series. A freelance journalist since 1992, she is a regular contributor to USA Today and USA Today Baseball Weekly. Her work also has appeared in the Chicago Tribune, Inside Sports, and ESPN Total Sports Magazine.